SCIENCE EXPLORER JUNIOR

Think Like a Scientist in the Backyard

by Matt Mullins

CHERRY LAKE PUBLISHING · ANN ARBOR, MICHIGAN

Published in the United States of America by Cherry Lake Publishing
Ann Arbor, Michigan
www.cherrylakepublishing.com

Content Editor: Robert Wolffe, EdD, Professor of Teacher Education,
Bradley University, Peoria, Illinois

Design and Illustration: The Design Lab

Photo Credits: Page 5, ©Mandy Godbehear/Shutterstock, Inc.; page 8,
©Dmitriy Shironosov/Shutterstock, Inc.; page 9, ©netbritish/Shutterstock,
Inc.; page 12, ©Old Paper Studios/Alamy; page 17, ©silver-john/
Shutterstock, Inc.; page 18, ©Panos Karapanagiotis/Shutterstock, Inc.;
page 23, ©Serg Zastavkin/Shutterstock, Inc.; page 24, ©sydeen/
Shutterstock, Inc.; page 28, ©Eti Swinford/Dreamstime.com; page 29,
©Monkey Business Images/Shutterstock, Inc.

Library of Congress Cataloging-in-Publication Data
Mullins, Matt.
  Think like a scientist in the backyard/by Matt Mullins.
      p. cm.—(Science explorer junior)
  Includes index.
  ISBN-13: 978-1-61080-167-6 (lib. bdg.)
  ISBN-10: 1-61080-167-9 (lib. bdg.)
  1. Meteorology—Juvenile literature. 2. Plants—Juvenile literature. I. Title.
  QC863.5.M853 2011
  551.5—dc22   2011006973

Cherry Lake Publishing would like to acknowledge the work
of The Partnership for 21st Century Skills. Please visit
www.21stcenturyskills.org for more information.

Printed in the United States of America
Corporate Graphics Inc.
July 2011
CLFA09

TABLE OF CONTENTS

How Does That Work?

Do you have questions about things you have seen in your backyard?

Have you ever looked at something and wondered, "How does that work?" Scientists do that all the time. Even in their backyards.

You can learn about physics by playing with a ball in your backyard.

Backyards are wonderful for playing with friends and eating with family. You can learn a lot about science in the backyard, too. How can we tell if we need a jacket today? Where does rain come from? How did that plant get over there? Scientists study **biology** and **physics** to answer these questions. You can study science, too—in your backyard!

STEP-BY-STEP

You can get your own answers by thinking like a scientist. Go step by step. You may have to repeat some steps as you go.

1. Observe what is going on.
2. Ask a question.
3. Guess the answer. This is called a **hypothesis**.
4. Design an experiment to test your idea.
5. Gather materials to test your idea.
6. Write down what happens.
7. Make a conclusion.

Don't forget your note pad!

Use words and numbers to write down what you've learned. It's okay if your experiment doesn't work. Try changing something, and then do the experiment again.

Always record your observations.

GET THE FACTS

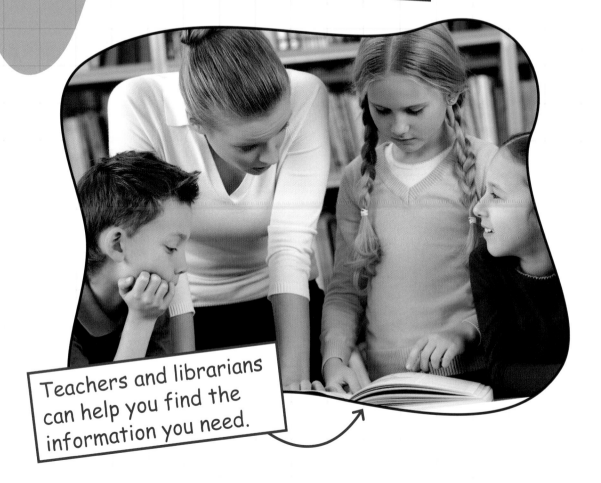

Teachers and librarians can help you find the information you need.

Scientists look for facts before they start an experiment. They use this information as a place to start.

Where can you find information? A library is filled with books, magazines, and science videos that can help you. You can talk to a teacher or a parent. You can visit a museum, too.

You can also find facts on the Internet. Be careful. Not everything on the Internet is the truth. Ask an adult to help you find the best places to look for information.

The Internet can also be a helpful research tool.

Make a Thermometer

The weather changes from day to day.

When we step into the backyard, one of the first things we notice is the weather. We look toward the sun. On a bright day, it might be warm outside. On a cloudy day, it might be a little cool.

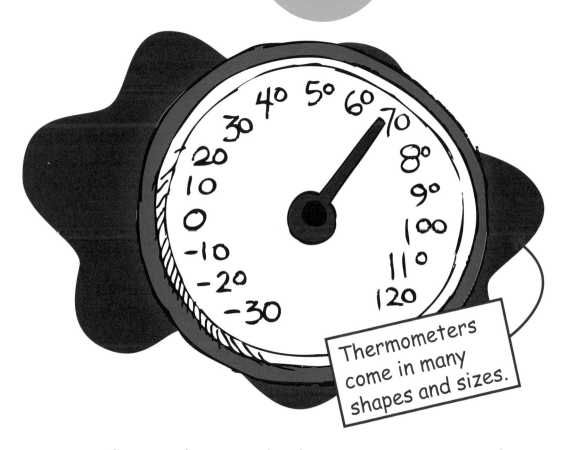

Thermometers come in many shapes and sizes.

How do you know whether or not you need to wear a coat to go into the backyard? If it's snowing or raining, that's easy. Sometimes you can check the temperature on a thermometer.

In the 1630s, a scientist named Robert Fludd had an idea. He knew that air expands when it is warm. Fludd thought he could make a thermometer with air and water in it. He put marks on a glass tube.

On one end of his tube was a bulb that held air. The other end was open.

Robert Fludd's thermometer helped scientists to make many new discoveries.

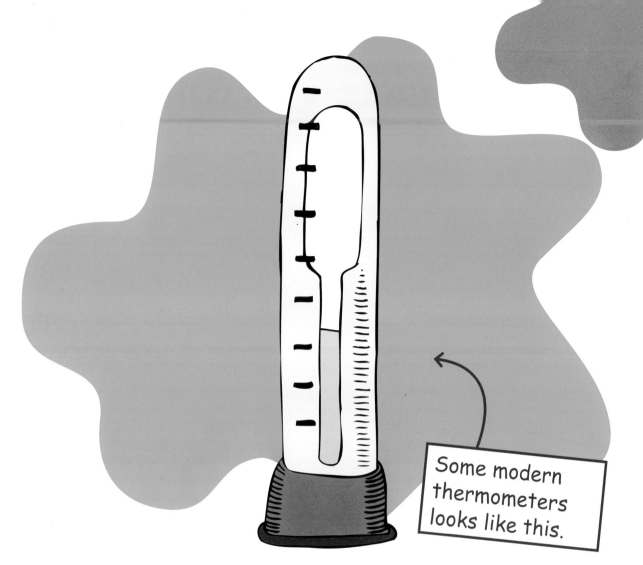

Some modern thermometers looks like this.

Fludd stood the tube up in a pitcher of water. He watched water rise up into the tube. Then Fludd set the pitcher with the thermometer outside. As the sun warmed the bulb, it warmed the air inside. As the air warmed up, it expanded to take up more room and pushed the water down. The marks on the tube indicated how much the temperature had changed!

DO AN EXPERIMENT

Be sure to remove any labels from the bottle before you start.

Red

You can make your own thermometer! Let's see if we can get air and water to move in a tube as the temperature changes. Fill a 16-ounce (473-milliliter) plastic bottle with warm water. Add a few drops of food coloring to it. Put a clear straw into the water, about one-third of the way in.

Use some clay to seal the bottle closed with the straw standing up. You will see water climb the straw. Mark the spot on the straw where the water stops. Now put the bottle in a bowl of ice. What happens to the water level? Is the temperature going down or up? What do you conclude about the effect of ice on the temperature of water?

Make sure the bottle doesn't tip over.

Evaporate It

Water bottles get cloudy as they heat up.

Have you ever left a closed, half-full bottle of water in the backyard? If you leave one outside for days, it may look different when you see it again. Water will bead up on the inside of the top half of the bottle.

How did the water get from the bottom of the bottle to the top? One of the things that happens is that water changes when it warms up. It turns to **gas**, or **vapor**. If something stops it from rising into the air, it turns to liquid water again.

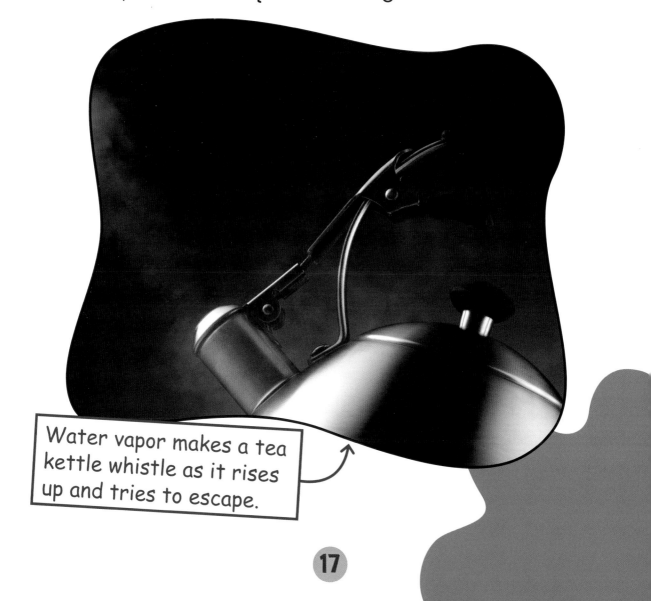

Water vapor makes a tea kettle whistle as it rises up and tries to escape.

Long ago, Aristotle had an idea about rain. He thought that water in oceans, lakes, and rivers evaporates. He said that it goes into the air as vapor. Then it comes back down as rain. If it's really cold, it will come down as snow, hail, or sleet! This is the **water cycle**. It is an important part of the way Earth's weather works.

Aristotle figured out the water cycle more than 2,000 years ago.

Use 2 tablespoons of salt.

You can use the process of **evaporation** to make rain. Evaporation can even make salt water become clean water! Get a deep bowl. Stir 2 cups (473 ml) of water and 2 tablespoons (28 grams) of salt together in the bowl. Keep stirring until you can't see the salt. Taste the mixture with your finger. It's okay to taste because you know what you put in the water. It's salty, right?

Now place a short, wide jar or cup in the bowl. The cup should not be as tall as the bowl. Ask an adult to help you cover the bowl with plastic wrap. Seal it tight! Put a small stone on top of the plastic wrap above the cup. The plastic should dip toward the cup but not be touching it. Set the wrapped bowl with the stone on top outside in the sun. Wait for 1 day.

What did you see when you went back to look at your experiment? Did the water evaporate and get stuck on the plastic? Did it roll down into the cup? Stick your finger in the cup with water in it. Taste the water. Is it salty, or is it plain? What do you conclude about evaporation?

Sock It!

Are there any flowers in your yard?

Backyards often have a lot of different plants in them. There is usually grass. There might be trees. Maybe you see shrubs. Maybe you see weeds. Maybe you have a garden. Are there more plants in your backyard than you can count with your fingers?

ASK A QUESTION

Sometimes plants grow in places we don't put them. Have you ever wondered how they get there? Many plants have seeds designed to travel. The plants drop seeds to the ground. Sometimes seeds get blown around by wind, like dandelion seeds. Sometimes animals move them.

Try blowing on a dandelion to see how the wind spreads its seeds.

DO THE RESEARCH

Seeds travel in many ways. In 1949, a scientist named E.J.H. Corner published a book. He had an idea about how an Asian fruit tree called the durian spread. He said that animals liked to eat the fruit. They carried the seeds in their bodies. When the animals left their dung, they left the seeds on the ground. New trees grew from the seeds!

The durian smells bad, but many people think it is very tasty.

DO AN EXPERIMENT

Seeds will stick to your socks.

Maybe you can find wild seeds and grow them somewhere else. Late summer and early fall are the best times for this experiment. Ask a parent for an old, fuzzy sock. Pull that sock on over your shoe. Then go out and play in your backyard. Or play at a park. Find a place with a lot of plants.

When you get back home, remove your sock. What do you see stuck to it? Get a milk carton or cut the top from a plastic jug. Put some soil in the bottom of the container. Ask an adult to help you cut open the sock so it can lie flat. Lay it on the soil in the container with the grass and seeds sticking up. Cover the sock with soil. Water it. Leave it outside in the sun.

What happens after a few days? Are you growing plants from wild seeds? Do you think seeds can get stuck to other things like they did to your sock? What can you conclude about how seeds travel?

What kinds of plants grow from the seeds?

Your Big Idea!

You can use a rain gauge to measure how much rain falls in your backyard.

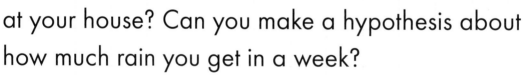

Remember how you made your own rain with water, a bowl, and plastic wrap? Why not measure how much rain you get at your house? Can you make a hypothesis about how much rain you get in a week?

Test your hypothesis with a rain gauge. Get a jar with a wide mouth. Place this in the backyard in a spot under the open sky. Every time it rains, pour the rainwater from your jar into a measuring cup. Write down how much rain fell that week. After 7 days, add up all of the rainfall amounts. That is your weekly rainfall total.

Did you guess correctly? Do you think your results would be different if you measured the rainfall for another week?

You can do a lot of science in your backyard!

What will your next backyard experiment be?

GLOSSARY

biology (bye-AH-luh-jee) the study of living things, including plants and animals

conclusion (kuhn-KLOO-zhuhn) the answer or result of an experiment

evaporation (i-vap-uh-RAY-shuhn) the way a liquid warms up and turns into gas

experiment (ik-SPER-uh-ment) a test of your idea

gas (GAS) a substance that fills whatever container you put it in

hypothesis (hye-PAH-thi-sis) a guess

physics (FIZ-iks) the science of matter and energy

thermometer (thur-MAH-mi-tur) a tool for measuring temperature

vapor (VAY-pur) another word for gas

water cycle (WAW-tur SYE-kuhl) the natural cycle of ice melt, pooling, evaporation, and rain

FOR MORE INFORMATION

BOOKS

Becker, Helaine. *Science on the Loose: Amazing Activities and Science Facts You'll Never Believe*. Toronto: Maple Tree Press, 2008.

Levine, Shar, Leslie Johnstone. *Backyard Science*. New York: Sterling Publishing Company, 2005.

WEB SITES

CSIRO: Do-It-Yourself Science
www.csiro.au/resources/DIYScience.html
Visit this site for links to a lot of fun science activities.

Family Education: Backyard Science Activities for Kids
fun.familyeducation.com/hobbies-and-interests/childrens-science-activities/32820.html
Discover quizzes to test your science skills and links to more activities you can do in your backyard.

INDEX

ABOUT THE AUTHOR

Matt Mullins holds a master's degree in the history of science. Matt lives in Madison, Wisconsin, with his son. Formerly a journalist, Matt writes about science, technology, and other topics, and writes and directs short films.